It was the middle of the night but Jake couldn't sleep.

3

Then something,
        somewhere, went **bump!**

"Help!" said Jake. "I'm scared!"

The Night Knight

Written by Timothy Knapman

Illustrated by Steve May

OXFORD
UNIVERSITY PRESS

OXFORD

UNIVERSITY PRESS

Great Clarendon Street, Oxford, OX2 6DP, United Kingdom

Oxford University Press is a department of the University
of Oxford. It furthers the University's objective of excellence
in research, scholarship, and education by publishing
worldwide. Oxford is a registered trade mark of Oxford
University Press in the UK and in certain other countries

Text © Timothy Knapman 2017
Illustrations © Steve May 2017
Inside cover notes written by Teresa Heapy

The moral rights of the author have been asserted

First published 2017

British Library Cataloguing in Publication Data
Data available

ISBN: 978-0-19-841514-5

10 9 8 7 6

Paper used in the production of this book is a natural, recyclable product
made from wood grown in sustainable forests. The manufacturing process
conforms to the environmental regulations of the country of origin.

Printed in China by Shanghai Offset Printing Products Ltd

Acknowledgements

Series Editor: Nikki Gamble

There was a flash and suddenly ...

... there was a knight in Jake's bedroom. He looked very brave.

"I am the Night Knight!" he said.
"I look after children when it's dark."

Then something,
somewhere, went **bump** again.

"Help!" said the knight. "I'm scared!"

"But it's your job to look after *me*!" said Jake. "Please go and see what's making the noise."

"Only if you come, too," said the knight.

So Jake held the knight's hand
to help him feel braver.

They walked around the dark house
together, looking for the **bump.**

"It's coming from that room," said the knight.

They went inside and saw ...

... a giant shadow in the moonlight!

"It's a big, scary monster!" said the Night Knight.

Then Jake looked closer.

"It's only Fluffy, my hamster," said Jake. "He's running on his wheel. Go to sleep, Fluffy!"

Soon the house was quiet.

Then something,
somewhere, went
**rumble
grumble!**

"Help!" said the Night Knight. "I'm scared!"

"But it's your job to look after *me*!" said Jake. "Please go and see what's making the noise."

"OK. But only if you come, too," said the knight.

So they walked around the dark
house together, looking for the
rumble grumble.

The **rumble grumble** was coming from Mum's room.

"It's a big, scary monster!" said the knight.

He tried to run away but he tripped over his shield.

Ouch!

Then Jake looked closer.

"It's only my mum, snoring," said Jake.
"Turn over, Mum!"

Soon the house was quiet again.

Then something, somewhere, went **squeaky creak!**

"Help!" said the Night Knight. "I'm scared!"

He tried to run away but he tripped over his cape.

"Your armour is squeaking," said Jake. "You just need some oil."

Soon the house was quiet again.

"You see?" said Jake. "There's nothing to be scared of."

"Thank you," said the Night Knight. "I feel much braver now."

Jake was very tired. He went back to bed. He said, "Night night," to the Night Knight.

Soon Jake was fast asleep. And the Night Knight looked after him until morning.